Child Millionaire

STOCK MARKET INVESTING FOR BEGINNERS

How to Build Wealth the Smart Way for Your Child

THE BASIC LITTLE GUIDE

ALEX NKENCHOR UWAJEH

Child Millionaire: Stock Market Investing for Beginners - How to Build Wealth the Smart Way for Your Child - The Basic Little Guide

By

Alex Nkenchor Uwajeh

Wisdom Quotes:

As long as the earth continues, there will always be a time for planting and a time for harvest. There will always be cold and hot, summer and winter, day and night on earth.

A wise youth harvests in the summer,

but one who sleeps during harvest is a disgrace.

A good person leaves an inheritance to his children's children.

Child Millionaire
STOCK MARKET INVESTING FOR BEGINNERS

Contents

Introduction

Have you ever considered starting up a savings account for your child's future? Perhaps you've thought about creating a savings plan to help pay for their education?

Can you imagine setting up your children's financial future so they'll never have to worry about the Government cutting their Social Security? They won't need to concern themselves with student debts to cover their education costs. They'll also never have to worry about collecting food stamps or being evicted from their home.

Most parents think about ways to make their children's financial lives a little easier as they grow up.

The primary reason so many parents don't do anything about setting up their children's financial future is simply because they don't know where to start.

Our schooling system doesn't focus on teaching students how to create wealth. Kids also aren't taught to save money or to work on a budget. Those lessons are left to parents to teach their kids as they grow up.

In fact, the school curriculum barely touches on the biggest contributing factor to growing wealth over time.

That factor is compound interest.

You see, even very small contributions from you have the power to grow into enormous amounts of money over time, thanks to the power of compounding. Yet the average person doesn't really understand how it's possible to earn interest on the interest you've already earned. It's also equally

possible to earn dividends on the dividends you've already earned.

Even if you only have small amounts to invest into your child's account, you can take advantage of compounding to grow those funds into a large amount of money over time.

The key is to create a strategy that maximizes the amount of money you contribute. If you're serious about building real wealth for your child's future, there are some simple steps you can take to make that goal into a reality.

Are you ready to get started?

Investing in the Stock Market

How much did you spend on your child's birthday gifts or Christmas gifts last year? Many parents spend a small fortune on stuffed toys, electronic gadgets, game consoles and other random things they think their kids might enjoy. Sure, the kids might get some entertainment value out of those things for a short time, but they're also quickly forgotten.

Imagine if you spent some of that money buying stocks for your children's future instead.

Buying one share of a blue-chip stock now while your child is young may not seem like a big contribution to their financial future. But the value of the stock may increase dramatically over time.
That single little stock you purchased for your child's first birthday could be worth 10 or 20

or even 100 times the original value by the time they turn 18.

As an example, when Apple stocks went public they were worth just $2.75 per share. Today you'll pay just under $104 per share for the same Apple stock.

Now imagine if you purchased one new stock for your child's portfolio each year and saw that same kind of growth over the years.

Over time, the value of the entire portfolio should increase simply due to the rise in share values. The initial investment from you should be relatively small, but the value to your child's financial future could be enormous.

By the time you finish this book, you'll also see there are other things you can do to increase your child's investment portfolio with very little extra effort from you.

Buying Stocks for a Child

Before you rush out and buy stocks in your own name, take some time to set up the correct accounts. If you purchase stocks in your name, they're yours. Even if you intended to buy them for your kids, if they're in your name, you're the legal owner.

In order for your kids to get the benefits, you may need to open a custodial account in your children's names. You can do this via your stock brokerage company by providing the child's personal information and social security number.

Even though the account is in your child's name, you will remain in full control of the account until the child turns 18. In some states, control remains with you until your child turns 21, so it pays to check when they're able to access their stocks.

Many brokerage firms offer custodial accounts that let you start buying stocks with very low minimums. If you shop around, you should also find accounts that won't charge you any set-up fees or any annual fees.

It's also worth comparing the commissions payable for buying and selling shares within the custodial account. The fees you pay for each online stock trade will differ between firms, so it's best to look at the options available and choose the one that best suits your plans and goals for your children. After all, you don't want your investments to be eaten away with unnecessary fees if you can avoid them.

Once your child's custodial brokerage account is operating you can go ahead and choose which stocks you want to add to your child's portfolio.

You will need to contribute some cash into the account in order to begin buying stocks, just as you would with a regular stock trading account.

Alternatively, if you have your own stocks in a brokerage account, you could choose to transfer stocks you already own over to your child's custodial account.

Any stock you transfer over will immediately become your child's property. This means your child will become responsible for paying tax on any

dividends or on any capital gains produced by the stocks in the custodial account.

Of course, if your child is still a minor they'll be subject to the 'kiddie tax' rules. We'll go through some of the basics about tax on a child's investment income a bit later in this book.

Direct Investment Plans

Some companies offer stock holders the option of a direct investment plan, or direct stock plan. This allows you to buy stock directly from the company through their transfer agents into your child's custodial account. You bypass the brokerage firm and avoid paying any commission costs, which can represent a significant saving.

Opting to purchase stocks directly from the company can be ideal if you only have a small amount of money to invest each month. You don't have to worry about your contributions to your child's portfolio being eaten away by brokerage fees.

Direct investment plans can also be a good option for those parents who are just beginning their child's investment portfolio.

As an example, you could choose to contribute $50 per month to a transfer agent to purchase a company's stock in your child's custodial account. The funds are debited by the transfer agent automatically from your nominated bank account each month. Those funds are then used to purchase new stocks for your child's custodial account.

You pay no commissions or brokerage fees, so your money is purchasing the maximum number of stocks allowable for your contribution.

While there are plenty of companies out there that will allow you to purchase stocks directly through their transfer agents, they're not always easy to find.

Perhaps the easiest way to start a direct investment plan is to select the stock you want to buy. Head over to the company's website and see if you can find a link for the FAQ page.

Check the FAQ list and see if you can find anything relating to purchasing stock directly from the company. If they do offer the option, you should be given a link pointing you to their transfer agent. If they don't offer the option, there should be a statement there somewhere letting you know that it's not available.

Head to the stock transfer agent's website and look for any information relating to the direct stock purchase plan for the company you want to invest in.

Remember, you're purchasing stock for your child's custodial account, but the money will be debited from your own bank account to fund the stock purchase. Be sure you enter the correct account information or you could end up buying stocks for yourself instead of your kids.

It's up to you whether you choose to make a one-time purchase or whether you want to set up a monthly investment plan for a specific amount of money.

Reinvesting Dividends

When most people think about investing in stocks, they immediately ponder the potential growth in value those stocks might incur over time. If you're working towards creating wealth for your child, seeing an increase in stock values over time is definitely an advantage.

However, there are other benefits you might be overlooking in terms of your wealth-building strategy.

You see, if you choose your stocks wisely, it's very possible to earn dividend income from them. The company whose stock you own will divide some of their profits among its shareholders and pay them in the form of dividends.

Many retirees choose to use those dividends to supplement their retirement incomes.

Yet when you're actively trying to build wealth for your child's future, you have the option of

reinvesting those dividends to boost the overall value of the stock portfolio.

For example, your child might receive a total of $100 in dividend income each year. That income could be used to purchase new stocks to keep the investment portfolio growing.

You have the option to purchase more of the same stock, or you can choose to diversify your child's investment portfolio to purchase shares in different companies stocks.

DRIP (Dividend Reinvestment Plan)

As an alternative option to investing the dividend cash you receive, you can elect to have your dividends automatically reinvested into a DRIP – or **Dividend Reinvestment Plan**.

Whenever dividends are due to be paid to shareholders, you can elect to have those dividends paid to your child in the form of stocks instead of

cash. The company in which you own shares of stock will calculate how much is due and then convert the dividend amount into an equivalent number of stocks.

For example, if your child has 10 shares of Company XYZ in his portfolio and the dividend due is 10%, your child will receive 1 share of stock. That new share is added to the existing portfolio.

In the event that the amount of dividend payment due isn't enough to cover the cost of a single share of stock, many companies will issue fractional shares.

For example, your child's share statements may show ownership of 12.135 shares. The fractional share amount is equivalent to the amount that would have been received if you had chosen to receive the dividends in the form of cash. When it's time to calculate the dividends due next year, the fractional share amount is also included in calculations.

Through the Dividend Reinvestment Plan, the number of shares within the portfolio increases each

year, but you're not paying any more of your own money to make it happen. It's an easy, automatic way to boost how many shares your child owns year after year.

You're also not paying brokerage fees for buying more stocks, as the company allocates the new shares as part of the Dividend Reinvestment Plan. They're simply added to your child's custodial brokerage account.

Over time, the number of shares owned in your child's portfolio keeps increasing as the company issues more stocks to the account. The value of each individual share of stock can also increase over time, boosting the overall value of the investment portfolio.

Your child's portfolio receives a double benefit:

- ★ **Additional stocks that cost you nothing out of your pocket**
- ★ **Capital growth in the value of each share**

These factors allow your initial investment to compound over time, which is the key to developing a successful investment plan for your child's future.

The best part about choosing a Dividend Reinvestment Plan is that you get to take full advantage of the power of compounding. The dividends earned might only amount to one additional share this year, but they could amount to 1.5 shares the following year and 2 shares the year after that.

The calculations used to work out how much to pay each shareholder in dividends is based on the number of shares owned. After a while, some of the shares in your kid's portfolio will have been received from previous dividend payments.

Essentially, your child is earning dividends from the dividends already received in previous years, thanks to the power of compounding.

Choosing a Millionaire Stock Portfolio

Choosing the right stocks to add to your child's stock portfolio can be challenging for many people. Obviously, you want to pick stocks that are likely to increase your child's wealth over the long term. At the same time, you don't want to run the risk of picking absolute losers.

So how do you know which ones to pick?

Many new investors believe that buying cheap stocks is a good way to increase the number of shares held in the custodial account overall. However, buying cheap stocks doesn't necessarily mean you're buying good value for money.

Many of the world's most successful investors spend time considering the company behind the stocks. Stocks in solid companies with a long track record of successful trading tend to be more expensive to buy initially, but they may also represent better long term investment.

Likewise, many successful investors research the rate of return they'll get from their investments in dividends. The actual dividends payable will differ from company to company.

If your strategy is to grow your child's stock portfolio using the Dividend Reinvestment Plan, it makes sense to choose stocks that pay a decent dividend amount per share owned each year.

If your strategy is to focus on potential capital growth of stocks owned, choose good companies with a solid future and strong management.

Information relating to any publicly listed companies is easy to obtain. Spend some time doing a little research before you make your stock purchase decisions.

Diversifying Your Child's Stock Portfolio

Buying a few carefully selected shares of a particular company's stock is a great start for your child's future. Selecting the Dividend Reinvestment Plan

option is also an ideal way to grow the number of shares within the portfolio on auto-pilot.

However, in order to protect your child's financial future, you may want to consider diversifying the types of shares you put into the portfolio.

Some investors advise choosing stocks across several different industries or market sectors. For example, you might buy shares of stock in a large bank one year and buy stock in a mining company the following and buy stock in a national retail company the next.

Imagine buying all your stocks in just the banking sector and nothing else. If something happened to reduce the value of stocks in the banking sector, your child's investment portfolio is wiped out.

Broadening your exposure to the types of stocks you hold in your child's portfolio can help to create a buffer against the market falling in any particular sector.

There's also the possibility of expanding your investing strategy to include different asset classes. For example, you may decide to contribute some cash into buying stocks and some cash into bonds, managed funds, savings accounts, precious metals or other asset types.

Diversifying an investment portfolio helps to minimize the risk of incurring losses if something happens in the market.

Index Funds

Some experts recommend choosing shares in Index Funds. For example, the NYSE Composite is an Index Fund that tracks the movement of the stock market. This is done by grouping together more than 2,000 common stocks listed on the New York Stock exchange and then tracking their movements.

There are lots of different Index Funds to choose from. For example, you might choose to invest in the Dow Jones Industrial Average or the Standard & Poors 500 or even the Nasdaq Composite.

Purchasing stocks in just one company means your share value can rise or fall depending on the performance of that single company. Investing in an Index Fund gives you much broader market exposure, which can help to minimize potential losses.

For example, you might invest $200 into an Index Fund and gain a very small stock holding in every one of the companies within that fund.

Investing in Index Funds may also offer a lower-cost option for starting your child's stock portfolio. These types of funds often have low operating expenses, as they're not paying incomes for highly-paid fund managers to pick stocks.

Keeping your operating costs low means you're maximizing the potential returns within your child's stock portfolio.

Penny Stocks vs Blue-Chip Stocks

Lots of investors are drawn to penny stocks as a way to buy a large number of shares at a relatively low price. The lure of buying stocks at a price of less than $1 each can be very appealing.

By comparison, buying one single share in a large blue-chip company can often cost a few hundred dollars. Many investors cringe at the idea of paying so much money for one single share of stock when it's possible to buy hundreds or even thousands of shares in another company for the same money.

What those investors might be overlooking is that the companies offering penny stocks are often small businesses seeking capital from investors. They may not even pay dividends at all, as the company you're investing may want to keep profits for future company growth, or they simply might not be making a profit at all yet.

There's absolutely no guarantee that the value of any stock you buy will go up or down. If you buy cheap

stocks in the hope they'll increase in value, you're investing in speculation.

However, when you invest in a company that pays good dividends per share owned, you automatically have a way to increase the value of your portfolio. Even if the value of each share stays the same, you get the benefit of earning dividends, which improves your returns right away.

Before you jump in and buy stocks based on what you believe is a cheap price, take a moment to think about the future of the company behind those shares. In order for your child to see the real benefits of your investing efforts, the companies you invest in will need to offer some form of returns over the long term.

Make Investing in Stocks Fun

While your child is still young, he may not even be aware of what you're buying. The stocks you choose should be for quality companies with a long-term track record.

However, as kids get older you might want to encourage them to participate in your stock selections.

In order to get your kids interested in their investment portfolio, try to select stocks they can relate to. For example, companies like Johnson and Johnson, Wal-Mart, Coca-Cola, Nike, Apple, McDonalds, Nintendo, Disney, or Dreamworks Animation are companies that most kids might associate with.

They know the products and they know the brand names. Explain to your kids that owning shares of stock in that company makes them a part-owner of the company. When the dividend statements arrive, explain that they're receiving their share of the company profits, just like every other shareholder in that company.

When your kids recognize and relate to a particular company, watching the performance of their stocks becomes more fun. Kids are also more likely to compare the performance of their favorite stocks to

the ones you might have picked for them when they were younger.

For example, you may have picked up stocks in the NYSE Composite Index Fund while your child was only 3 years old. You might also have purchased stocks in Bank of America when the child was 4, stocks in a large pharmaceutical company when he was 5.

By the time your child is 9, they may be interested in purchasing stocks in McDonalds or Coca-Cola. What matters here is that they're showing an interest in how the whole stock investment idea is catching on in their minds.

There's no harm in buying one or two shares of stock in a company your kids can relate to. You're making their investment journey fun and they're learning how the process works. After all, once your kid turns 18 he'll be expected to handle his investment decisions responsibly on his own, so it's best to make the process fun and interesting wherever you can.

Besides, you can always contribute your own stock selections to your child's account to keep the portfolio balanced if you're worried about their choices.

High Interest Savings Account

Investing in stocks is a great way to build wealth for your children's future. When you compare the returns on stock investments to the interest paid on savings accounts, it's easy to see why so many people are turning to the stock market.

With interest rates so low, leaving your cash sitting in the bank may not be the most exciting way to grow wealth. In fact, at interest rates of around 1%, it's quite disheartening to see such low returns on your cash.

Yet cash still remains one of the safest investment options available.

You see, while the interest you earn might be far lower than the returns available in other markets, it is a guaranteed return. The returns on the stock

market are never guaranteed, regardless of which stocks you purchase.

Perhaps the biggest benefit to opening a high interest savings account for your child is teaching them the value of saving money. The habit of saving is an important skill all kids will take with them into adulthood.

The good old piggy bank still has value in a child's eyes. Money in a piggy bank is a real, tangible way for them to see their money growing. Encourage them to put aside their spare change or loose coins into a piggy bank.

When it's full, count out your coins and make a trip to the bank. Some banks even offer coin-counting machines in the branch that let kids see how much all those coins are worth after they're counted. Let the kids know why the money goes into the bank once the piggy bank is full and work on ways to explain the concept of earning interest on their savings.

When your kids see the interest payments accruing in their savings account, you can explain to them that the bank pays them for leaving their savings in the account as a type of reward. Kids respond remarkably well to positive rewards, even when it's only in the form of a couple of dollars.

Even at an interest rate of 1%, the power of compounding can still grow wealth for your child over time. You may have managed to contribute $1,000 into your child's savings account. At a 1% interest rate, you should earn $10 in interest even if you didn't contribute any additional funds.

If you were to contribute just $20 per month into your child's savings account on top of that initial $1,000, you would have saved more than $5,044 in 15 years. $444 of that sum comes from interest earned on the account.

Imagine if you contributed $100 per month during that same 15 year period. Your child would have $20,573. $1,573 of that amount would have been earned in interest.

Earning some extra cash by doing chores or taking on a summer job can be a good way for kids to learn about earning income. Learning how to divide their income up into savings, investing and spending money is a valuable life-lesson that all kids can benefit from.

Many banks offer custodial savings accounts. You can open an account in your child's name and contribute cash into it until they're old enough to start saving their own pocket money or part-time income.

Be sure you shop around among the banks, credit unions and financial institutions for the best interest rate you can find. You may also want to check what account fees may apply.

It's also a good idea to check how frequently the interest is paid. Some banks calculate interest on the account balance on a daily basis, but don't pay the interest due until the end of the month. Other accounts calculate interest monthly.

For the purpose of compounding your child's savings, opting for an account that calculates interest daily will help grow the balance faster. The interest rates paid on savings won't be high, but it's still worth shopping for the best account you can find to help maximize the returns on your child's money.

Precious Metals: Silver and Gold

For a lot of people, precious metals represent a tangible asset. Kids can hold a gold coin and see what it looks like. By comparison, showing them a stock certificate or a bank statement doesn't hold the same thrill.

Investing in gold and silver can be a good way to protect against crashes in other investment markets. Historically, gold values have risen on average around 6-7% per year over the past twenty years or so. While the capital growth may not be as high as some other types of investments around, it's still a much healthier return on your investment compared to the interest paid on cash sitting in savings accounts.

Of course, owning precious metals won't earn any passive income, so you can't take advantage of the power of compounding. You can't earn interest on gold you own and you don't earn dividends from owning bullion or coins.

The primary reason for investing in silver and gold is the hope that the value of your precious metals increases over time.

You can buy gold and silver coins directly from the U.S. Mint. Buying them direct may be a cheaper way to start building your child's collection than buying them through coin dealers. When you buy directly from the Mint, you also know you're getting the real deal and not a lookalike version of a coin.

The U.S. Mint also offers bullion version of many collector's coins. If you prefer the idea of investing in the precious metal over the option of coin sets, bullion may be a good option.

Keep in mind that as your gold and silver collection grows, you have the challenge of finding secure storage for it. The cost of storing gold can be quite expensive, which could potentially wipe out any growth in value you hoped to achieve. Likewise, storing gold and silver in your home could expose you to the risk of theft, even if you keep it in a safe.

Precious metals should be considered an important part of a well-diversified investment portfolio for your child. While you're working out your strategy to grow your child's wealth, consider investing in gold and silver as part of your plan.

Roth IRA for Children

Adding a Roth IRA to your child's investment portfolio can be a great way to supercharge your child's wealth building strategy.

For adults, the benefit of investing into a Roth IRA is that you can grow your savings tax-free. Any profits made within your Roth IRA account are tax free and you also pay no taxes on any withdrawals you make from the account after retirement age.

However, the rules surrounding Roth IRA accounts for children are a little different. In order to successfully use a Roth IRA for your child's wealth building strategy, you will need to work around some of the rules and red-tape in order to see the real benefits.

One of the biggest advantages of investing into a Roth IRA while your kids are still young is the length of time the investments have to grow. The sheer power of compound interest allows even

modest investment amounts to grow to enormous amounts of money over time.

The younger your child is when you open a Roth IRA account, the more time you have for the power of compound interest to do its work in growing more wealth.

Overcoming Challenges to Setting up a Roth IRA for Children

The difficulty in opening a Roth IRA for children is that the child must have earned an income to qualify. You can't simply give your kid the money to invest as a gift, as that strategy won't work.

Your child needs to have earned an income and filed a tax return.

If your child is still only a baby, that might seem like a difficult challenge to overcome. But it's certainly not impossible.

Think about it this way: you might choose to have some of your child's stocks paying a dividend

income each year. That income will need to be reported and your child's small dividend income will be subject to the Kiddie Tax. Any remaining portion could then be contributed to the Roth IRA account.

There's also another alternative available. For example, let's assume you're self-employed and you own a dog grooming salon. Let's also assume your child is only 12 months old. While your baby can't work in your business directly, you could easily hire your baby as a model. Your newly-hired model can make appearances in brochures or on catalogues or other printed media. You can even hire your baby to appear in TV commercials to advertise your business.

Your business may be able to treat the expense as a tax deduction, but the money becomes income to your child. The IRS taxes your child's income at a much lower rate, and the remainder can be put into their Roth IRA.

As your child grows older, they can start accepting simple chores and tasks that allow them to earn extra

money on their own. If you own a business, there may be some simple chores they can do to assist, such as cleaning, filing, shoveling snow, baby sitting, weeding, mowing, or delivering leaflets around the local area.

When your child becomes a teenager, you can encourage him to get a part-time job on weekends or after school. Any income earned can either be put aside into savings or contributed into the Roth IRA to help boost the value even further.

If you've helped your child set up a Roth IRA and they've contributed some of their own income to it, you might be able to continue making some contributions for them. While you won't receive a tax break for the gift, your kids will certainly reap the benefits of your contribution in the future.

Kiddie Tax 101

The Kiddie Tax was introduced to discourage parents from shifting their investment income to their children in an effort to reduce their own taxes. As children are usually in a much lower tax bracket than their parents, it can be tempting for some parents to try and take advantage of the difference.

Kiddie Tax is applied to any unearned income greater than $2,000 for children up to the age of 18. However, some students may still fall under the Kiddie Tax rule up to the age of 23 in some circumstances.

If your child earns income from working, the Kiddie Tax will not apply. The tax will only apply to unearned income from investments, including interest on savings, dividends and capital gains.

The Kiddie Tax will only apply to your child once any investment income exceeds $2,000. If you're just starting out with your

child's investment strategy, you won't need to worry too much about it just yet.

However, as your child's portfolio grows you may need to report the investment income received. When the income from investments exceeds $2,000, it will need to be reported to the IRS.

The first $1,000 you report on your tax return will be considered tax free, while the second $1,000 will be taxed at the kid's rate. Any investment income above $2,000 is charged at the parent's marginal tax rate.

There are two ways to pay Kiddie Tax:

1. **Add your child's income to your own tax return**
2. **Complete a separate tax return for your child**

Remember that there may be implications to your own tax situation when reporting your child's income. If you're in any doubt about Kiddie Tax and how it might affect your child's investments or your own income, talk to a qualified accountant or tax agent about your situation. Ask plenty of questions and be sure you understand the responses you receive.

Letting Go of the Reins

While your kids are still very young, you are likely to be the person in charge of growing their wealth. You chose their initial stocks. You chose their bank accounts and you chose their investment strategy.

Over time, many kids will develop an interest in what you're doing. Be sure to explain as much as you can to them so they know why you're investing and what your goals are.

As they get older it's very important that your children understand how to manage their own money responsibly to keep your good intentions going. After all, if you manage their finances for them every step of the way and then hand them a large sum of money at the age of 18, chances are they won't know what to spend it on first!

Kids can benefit enormously by learning to control their own money at a young age. The lessons you teach them while they're very young about money and investing are likely to stay with them for

decades into the future, especially if you make the process fun.

Once they start earning their own income, your kids need to understand the benefit of breaking down their income into allocated portions. For instance, you might encourage them to put aside a percentage of any income earned into savings, another percentage goes into investing, and the rest is allocated to spending money.

Not only are you helping your children to develop strong money management skills while they're still young, but you're also teaching them valuable money habits that will last them a lifetime.

As your kids get older, they'll develop more confidence in their abilities to choose stocks and other investments on their own. Of course, most kids will still refer to you for advice or suggestions on what they should do next, but ultimately the decisions they make once you've let go of the reins need to be theirs.

Conclusion

Setting up an investment portfolio for your children really can be easier than most people expect. You don't need large amounts of money to get started and you don't need to spend lots of time building up the investments.

The real key to building wealth for your children is to start as soon as you can. Contribute whatever you can afford into your kid's investments and work on ways to leverage the power of compounding to your advantage.

After all, if you can set up your kid's portfolio so that it increases automatically – either by Dividend Reinvestment Plans or by earned interest or by capital growth – you have the benefit of time on your side.

By the time your kids turn 18, it's very likely they'll have a large amount of wealth put aside in their names. They should also have developed some excellent money skills throughout that time that

should help them create a strong financial future that will last them for a lifetime.

Warning: Prior to choosing where to invest your money, it is very important that you do some research.

Your capital is at risk when you invest in stocks - you can lose some or all of your money, so never risk more than you can afford to lose. Always seek professional advice if you are unsure about the suitability of any investment. Past performance is not a reliable indicator of future results.

Every attempt has been made to provide accurate, up to date and reliable complete information, no warranties of any kind are expressed or implied. Readers acknowledge that the author is not engaging in rendering legal, financial or professional advice.

The reader agrees that under no circumstances are we responsible for any losses, direct or indirect, which are incurred as a result of use of the

information contained within this book, including –
but not limited to errors, omissions, or inaccuracies.

Check Out Other Books:

Investing in Gold and Silver Bullion - The Ultimate
Safe Haven Investments

Nigerian Stock Market Investment: 2 Books with
Bonus Content

The Dividend Millionaire: Investing for Income and
Winning in the Stock Market

Economic Crisis: Surviving Global Currency Collapse - Safeguard Your Financial Future with Silver and Gold

Passionate about Stock Investing: The Quick Guide to Investing in the Stock Market

Guide to Investing in the Nigerian Stock Market

Building Wealth with Dividend Stocks in the Nigerian Stock Market (Dividends - Stocks Secret Weapon)

The Beginners Basic Guide to Investing in Gold and Silver Boxed Set

Beginners Basic Guide to Stock Market Investment Boxed Set

Precious Metals Investing For Beginners: The Quick Guide to Platinum and Palladium

Bitcoin and Digital Currency for Beginners: The Basic Little Guide

Stock Market Terms

Annual Report

A report that public companies are required to file annually. It describes past years' financial results and plans for the coming year. Annual reports include information about a company's assets,

liabilities, earnings, profits, and other year-end statistics.

Averaging: The process of gradually buying more and more securities in a declining market (or selling in a rising market) in order to level out the purchase (or sale) price.

Blue Chip: A company that has a history of solid earnings, regular and increasing dividends, and an impeccable balance sheet.

Breakout

When the price of a stock surpasses its initial high (resistance level) or falls below the initial low (support level), it is termed as break out in technical analysis.

Director Dealings

When directors buy or sell shares in their company.

Elliott Wave Theory: It assumes stock prices can be predicted by observing the various stages of waves that take place in its price cycle.

Oversubscribed

A company may offer for sale a certain number of shares. If applications are received for shares in excess of the number offered, the issue is termed as oversubscribed.

IPO - Initial Public Offering (IPO) is the announcement that the company is selling stock in itself for the first time.

If you would like to share this book with another person, please purchase an additional copy for each recipient. Thank you for respecting the hard work of this author.

www.ingramcontent.com/pod-product-compliance
Lightning Source LLC
Chambersburg PA
CBHW051247170526
45165CB00004B/1614